PRESENTS

THE DEFINITIVE GUIDE TO FORTNITE 2023

A TOTALLY INDEPENDENT PUBLICATION

Written by Naomi Berry
Designed by Jon Dalrymple

A Pillar Box Red Publication

© 2022. Published by Pillar Box Red Publishing Limited. Printed in the EU.

ISBN 978-1-914536-35-9

Images © Epic Games.

WELCOME

Fortnite has passed the five year mark, but doesn't it feel like it's been so much longer? The game has become such a huge, immovable behemoth in pop culture that it's hard to remember a time before the Battle Bus. It's almost harder to think of a future without it.

It's not an easy feat, you know, for a game to last that long. Most titles have a shelf-life of about 1-2 years, max (we are a fickle species, after all). But Fortnite has not only managed to ride the wave for over half a decade - they've rode right on the very top of that wave, doing the floss upon their surfboard.

Epic Games have managed to keep Fortnite fresh by pumping out continuous content to keep players entertained, landed some of the biggest collaborations in the gaming industry, and haven't been afraid to wipe the slate and start again: twice.

We're on Chapter 3 of Fortnite now, and while it may be shiny and new in a lot of ways, the fundamentals have remained the same. When it comes to Battle Royale, there are three keys to earning that all important Victory Royale: gathering, building and surviving. If you master these three basics, you'll be racking up Ws faster than a Quadcrasher cruising across an open field.

So flick this book open to whatever chapter you need, join a match, and I'll see you in that final 1v1 for the crown.

CONTENTS

GLOSSARY

Fortnite is bigger than ever, which means there's a whole new slew of terms that join a host of classics. Knowing your Ps from your Qs is useful for general play, but it's a definite must if you want to play in a team and communicate with your squad in the most effective way possible. We're on Fortnite's third chapter now; there's no excuse to be baffled on voice chat when your teammate shouts "He's been Harry Potter'ed in LeBron's House!" It's time to learn to speak Fortnite.

90S

A building technique pioneered by pros that requires a lot of practice. Check out the Building chapter (p. 14-17) for more details.

ADS

This is short for 'Aim Down Sights', which means to kinda zoom in to your shot for more accuracy. Use your right mouse click to do this.

AR

Short for 'assault rifle'.

BANDIES

Bandies is short term slang for bandages.

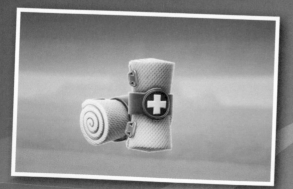

BIG POT

A common term used for the Rare Shield Potion.

BLANK

When you're sure you just shot an enemy but there's no damage registered due to a server issue.

BLOOM

A weapon's spray of bullets when fired. If a weapon has bloom, it means bullets can land essentially anywhere within their crosshair, which is less accurate than, say, a direct snipe. Bloom can be lessened by standing still or crouching when shooting.

THE BUBBLE

The circle of the map that is unaffected by the storm.

BOT

Technically, bot means an AI player, but it's usually used to describe human players that are so bad they're playing like they've been poorly programmed.

CRACKED

Converse to the above, if a player is described as cracked, it means they're highly skilled.

DOWNED/KNOCKED

A player whose HP has been depleted, but they can still be healed before they are finally eliminated.

DUB

Short for the letter 'W' (say it out loud if you can't see it), which is short for 'win'.

FARMING

Going out of your way to gather more building materials.

HARRY POTTER'ED

Used in verb form, when it comes to Fortnite - if a player is Harry Potter'ed, it means they're stuck under some stairs.

HEALS

Any item - from bandages right to fish - that provides health points.

HOT DROP

A hot drop is a major POI that is a popular landing spot.

LAUNCH

Shorthand for launch pads.

LEBRON'S HOUSE

A house with a basketball court.

LOADOUT

The items and weapons that you have in your arsenal.

MATS

Short for 'materials', i.e. wood, brick and metal.

MINIS

Used to refer to Small Shield Potions.

ONE/ONE-SHOT

If an enemy is 'one' or 'one-shot', then they're one shot away from being knocked. This is useful to communicate so teammates know whether to rush an enemy or take cover.

POI

Short for 'Point of Interest' - basically any named spot on the map, like Tilted Towers, Rocky Reels, Coney Crossroads, etc.

REZ

Short for 'resurrect', this often screamed shorthand is usually a plea from one of your teammates to help them with some heals before their health zeroes.

SHIELD POP

This call means that an opponent's shield has been either partially or fully destroyed.

SPAWN ISLAND

You're loaded onto this island while waiting for the next round of Battle Royale to start. The island regularly changes to reflect the season's theme, or tease upcoming changes.

QUICK SCOPE

Using ADS for the hottest of seconds to check accuracy before taking your shot.

TAG/TAGGED

Tagging means to deal a small amount of damage to an enemy player, or receiving a small amount of damage from an enemy.

WHITES

If a player is "on whites", it usually means they do not have any shields left. It can also mean using health potions that heal white health. If you notice, damage dealt with no shield is shown in white.

THE NEXT CHAPTER

When Chapter 2 came to a close at the hands of Dwayne "The Rock" Johnson (sure, why not), the well-loved and well-trodden island we all knew flipped upside down, revealing a whole new Battle Royale arena beneath and a brand new era: Chapter 3.

A NEW ISLAND

So to break the ice (sorry, we had to), players were greeted with a brand new island that required a good thaw. The wintry biome in the island's western half gave way to warmer climates to the east and south, with new locations and environments across a variety of biomes: snow, sea, desert and pasture.

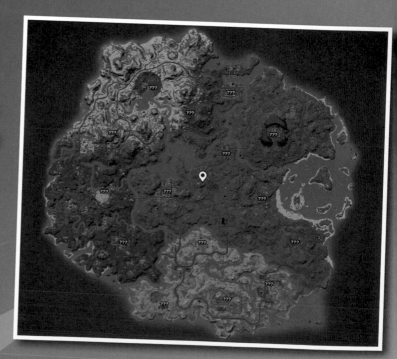

TIP!
Take a closer look at the new island on p. 44-47.

NEW MOBILITY

And with a new island came new ways to move around it. New methods of mobility range from traversing from A to B to combat maneuvers. Players can now slide down a hill while building or shooting to up their speed in duels, or even don Peter Parker's famed Spidey gloves to swing between buildings and cover bigger chunks of ground faster.

> ## TIP!
> **For more in-depth info on mobility, check out our chapter Map Mobility on p. 48-51.**

On top of that, players now have more mobility when in precarious situations like being knocked. If you're down but not out, you can now open doors and chests, crawl faster and access your inventory in order to up your chances of survival.

NEW PAST-TIMES

Chapter 3 also brought new hobbies to partake in, because hey - it's not all gunfire and rocket launchers out there. Sometimes you just want to kick back and take in the views of the beautiful island without worrying about your mortality for just a minute or two. Enter Chapter 3 camping.

Camping creates a home base for you to throw down a tent to heal or stash items. You can camp solo or share a site with your squad. If the storm's closing on your spot, you can leave your gear behind or pack up and take them with you, if you've got the time.

NEW BRAGGING RIGHTS

Bragging rights took on a whole new, tangible form in Chapter 3 with the introduction of the Victory Crown. Battle Royale winners bestowed with it are both blessed and somewhat cursed, because while it may be proof of first place, it's also a big ole' target on your back (or head, technically). Managing to hold on to the crown brings you bonus XP, and an emote (with your Battle Royale Victory count) if you win while wearing it. Heavy is the head that bears the crown, right?

NEW XP AVENUES

Speaking of XP, Chapter 3 opened up different methods of earning XP. Outside of Battle Royale, players can now earn XP in Creative Mode and Save the World to funnel into their Battle Pass. For more info on gaining XP, be sure to check out Making Progress on p. 54-55.

THE 3 BASICS:
GATHERING

Looking to be the last man standing? Simple. Just master the three basics of Fortnite: gathering, building and surviving.

The first basic you should master is the art (yep, it's an art) of gathering. Sure, your weapon arsenal and healing items are important parts of your loadout, but there's a reason why we're covering gathering first. Good gathering is key for good building, good building is key to survival, and survival is key to Victory Royale. Got it? It's a three-step process. So let's jump into step one.

TOOLS OF THE TRADE

Eventually you'll be swapping out sub-machine guns for rocket launchers, but when you first land on the island, it's just you and your Pickaxe. Your Pickaxe will be your most trusted friend. It might not have your back when it comes to combat (I mean, 20 damage per hit certainly isn't anything to write home about) but harvesting? That's where it shines.

THE MATS LIFE

Materials (more commonly known as just "mats") come in three forms: wood, stone and metal.

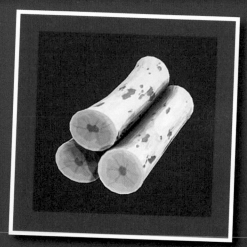

WOOD

The most common of mats, wood is both the easiest to find and the fastest to build with. The trade off? It's the weakest, so it's the fastest for an enemy to take down, too. Wood has pretty low HP, and is the only building mat that is flammable. As expected, wood can be found all across the island. You can harvest it from sources like:

- **Trees and Bushes:** It's rare you'll be in a biome that doesn't have them, but you can seek out orchards if you're looking for a quick way to max out. Pro tip! Never chop a tree all the way down - the animation might alert nearby players of your location.

- **Furniture:** If you land in a residential hotspot, be sure to chop up some of the house interiors and decoration on your way out to start your collection early.

- **Wooden Structures:** Wood is literally everywhere - fences, shacks, pallets, barricades... Find something on the island? Give it a whack, there's a good chance it'll pop out some logs.

STONE

The middleman of mats - it's both the second strongest and second fastest to build with. Stone is a pretty sturdy upgrade from wood, and it isn't flammable (but it can be damaged by nearby flames). It isn't quite as abundant as wood, but you'll still be able to gather more than enough if you look in the right places:

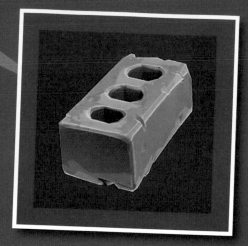

- **Boulders and Rocks:** These natural resources can be found in areas near water, like riverside and waterfalls.

- **Building Walls:** Tearing down a building wall will yield quite a fair bit of stone. Just don't rely on this method if you're trying to hotfoot it out of a hotspot landing; walls definitely aren't the fastest source to plunder.

- **Stone Structures:** Head to POIs like the Temple, the Ruins or Tumbledown Temple if you want to max out Stone quickly.

METAL

- **Metal is a double-edged mat:** It's by far the strongest, but also the slowest. With the highest mats HP, it's best used when you're building defensively if you've got downtime, or if you're really trying to turtle mid-battle in order to recover (provided you've bought yourself some shielded time with some stone first). You can harvest metal from:

- **Cars:** You don't have to hop into every car you see; they're a great source of metal. Just be careful of the alarms going off and alerting enemies to your position.

- **Wreckages:** You can find rusty wrecks in Rustaway Shores and Wreck Ravine, which are quick and easy metal sources.

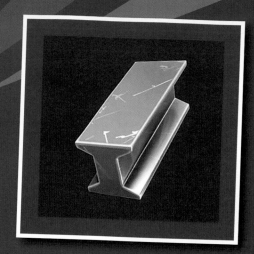

- **Metal Structures:** These are a little rarer than wooden structures, but you will find metal structures like fences, trailers, and shipping containers dotted around the island.

GATHER NOW, PROFIT LATER

You can harvest up to x999 pieces of each mat in Battle Royale (x500 in Arena), so never hesitate to stock up if you can. You'd be surprised how quickly you can tear through your reserves throughout a match, and especially during end-game duels.

You want to start gathering at the start of the match with the intention of saving it for later. Generally speaking, it's harder to find mats the further into a match you get - whether it's because other players have been snatching up sources or you're pressed for time to look when the bubble is shrinking and you're on the run, you'll be thanking yourself for stocking up on mats back in the good old days.

TIP!
Hotspots already ravaged by other players? Don't forget to keep an eye out for Chests, Supply Drops and Loot Llamas for mats. They're also a great pick-up reward after winning a duel.

THE 3 BASICS:
BUILDING

The second of the three basics to master in Fortnite is perhaps the trickiest: building. The building mechanic is what makes Fortnite stand out among a very crowded, very competitive Battle Royale genre. it's not enough to just shoot your way to a Victory Royale, you've also got to build yourself a platform up there above the slain bodies of your opponents.

Okay, maybe not that exactly - but you do need to know the fundamentals in order to increase your chances of making it to the end. The good news? You're already like... 15% of the way there if you've got your mats knowledge down. Hmm... that doesn't sound quite as reassuring when it's written out like that. Okay, real good news? You don't need to be at the level the pros are at, throwing up fifty storey towers in a 1v1 in the blink of an eye, complete with a launchpad on the top so when they land that killing blow, they can glide off into the sunset in a very satisfyingly cinematic fashion.

All you need to know are the building basics - just enough to rebalance gameplay to cater to your win conditions when things go wrong. Stuck in the storm? Build a tower and launch yourself out. Trying to move fast on difficult terrain? Build a bridge between literal mountain peaks. Found yourself in a 1v1? Build cover, build traps, box in your enemy or secure yourself a safe exit. See? Sounds a lot more doable, right?

TURBO MODE

First off, let's talk Turbo. Turbo Build is a configuration that lets you hold left-click (on PC, obviously) to build continuously via aim. If you're playing on console/with a controller, then you'll want to switch the configuration to Builder Pro. It'll make all things building a lot faster and a lot smoother.

KNOW YOUR MAT STATS

You know how it goes by now: like almost everything you can hit in Fortnite, mats have stats. There are four types of structures you can build, and each structure costs 10 mats from your inventory to construct, but that's where the commonalities stop.

So to translate all these numbers to layman terms: wood is weak but the best for emergencies (like negating fall damage, or making a speedy escape), metal is the best for hunkering down to turtle or making late-game structures, and stone... stone is right there in the middle, never the worst, never the best, and therefore likely never your first pick.

Material	Structure	Min HP	Max HP	Until Max HP (sec)
Wood	Wall	90	150	4
	Ramp, Roof, Floor	84	140	3.5
Stone	Wall	99	300	11.5
	Ramp, Roof, Floor	93	280	12
Metal	Wall	110	500	24.5
	Ramp, Roof, Floor	101	460	22.5

STRUCTURE TYPES

- **Walls:** A wall is your best defensive structure in that you can throw one up like a giant shield when someone starts shooting at you. If you know that a fight is on the way, you can also put one up preemptively and edit in a window as a vantage point to shoot from.

- **Ramps:** Ramps are the structure for mobility, allowing you to quickly gain the high ground during a 1v1 or make yourself a shortcut up to higher parts of the map.

- **Roofs:** Use roofs to provide cover from above if you're on the low ground taking damage, or to trap and box in an opponent during a build fight.

- **Floors:** Floors are good for direct map traversal to cut across an open area. It's also a good structure to put beneath you as you build upwards in order to provide cover.

These four structures are your basics, but the real game of Fortnite building is quick editing. Responsive, active edits are a huge part of Fortnite building: adding a trap for a pursuer, a door to make a sudden exit, or even deleting a floor to make a sudden drop ambush. Read your situation and build and edit accordingly.

FOUNDATIONAL THINKING

Like all real world structures, Fortnite builds require foundation. You can build literally whatever your heart desires, provided that it is anchored to the map at some point. Not only is this key to remember when you're building, but it's also key to remember when faced with an opponent's build: all it takes is a solid blow to the foundation for the whole thing to come crashing down.

- Avoid a catastrophe by beefing up your build with more than one foundational anchor. It gives multiple targets for an enemy to have to take down, and it gives you more time to set down new anchors where you're at or to make an escape.

- If you find yourself on the low ground during a build battle, don't bother trying to outpace them upwards; focus on locating key structural anchors to have their build come tumbling down.

- And if you happen to stumble across two people engaged in a build battle, then why not strike down their foundations and catch them by surprise? They likely didn't see you coming and there's a good chance the duel and the fall damage are going to put things in your favour when they land. Hey, don't waste free food.

> **TIP!**
>
> You can build anchors into the ground, against cliffs, mountains, hills and the sides of pre-existing structures and buildings.

BREAD AND BUTTER BUILDS

Creative is the place to really flex your architectural flair. When it comes to Battle Royale, there are really only four key builds you're going to be throwing up on Artemis. Master this quad and you'll have the competitive edge when it comes to building in a high pressure match scenario.

- **1x1:** The most basic of builds, the 1x1 is four walls and a ramp in the middle for some increased structural integrity. Build the ramp first (beneath your feet, obviously; you're not trying to Harry Potter yourself) and then place the walls around it with a little spin on the spot.

- **Ramp Rush:** Regular ramps get the ascension job done, but they're flimsy and very easy for an opponent to take out from beneath you. That's where a Ramp Rush comes in - it's essentially a reinforced ramp, with a wall built beneath each incline. The super strong version of the Ramp Rush also includes a floor (creating a kind of cheese wedge style triangle). Both versions will secure whatever ascent you're trying to make.

- **Turtle:** The turtle is your defensive go-to, a simple yet effective build to hunker down. It's essentially a 1x1 with an added roof, and sure, that doesn't sound like it's all that, but when you start placing them right next to each other and editing a pathway through... your enemy will be balling fists trying to break through them and find you. If you find yourself stuck on the lowground with no way to tip the scales, these are your best option.

- **90s:** We may be three chapters in, but 90s haven't gotten any less integral (or easier to throw up, unfortunately). 90s require countless 90-degree turns (see what they did there?) to build upwards: build a ramp and a wall, jump and turn 90 degrees, build a ramp and a wall, jump and turn 90 degrees, build a ramp and a wall... Yeah, you get it. These require really quick fingers to get right, but with practice, it becomes more of a muscle memory output than a conscious routine. And they're worth the trouble; by far 90s are the fastest way to gain reinforced height.

TIP!

If you want to practice your build skills without the threat of imminent assassination, pop into Battle Lab or Creative mode. You can practice throwing up 90s to your heart's content without worrying about anyone interrupting.

THE 3 BASICS:
SURVIVING - HEALTH AND SHIELDS

Building and Gathering are reasonably straightforward, but the third (and final) basic of Fortnite is a little more multi-faceted: survival. So let's start with the most integral part of survival - Health and Shields.

While it's instinctual to think Battle Royale is all about the fight, a huge part of survival (perhaps the biggest part) is about Health and Shield management. Think about it: you don't get eliminated for not having perfect aim or not knowing your way around the island - you get eliminated when your Health hits zero.

RESTORING HP

Healing methods have come and gone in Fortnite over the years, but the Healing mainstays have always been the following:

BANDAGES

The bread and butter of Fortnite's healing offerings, Bandages are a Common healing item that have been in the game since launch. They provide +15 HP (capped at 75 HP), and take three seconds to use.

MEDKIT

Medkits restore full health, but they trade off their potency with a massive 10 second application time. This means Medkits should be reserved for use only when you're sure you're safe. Trying to use one of these in the middle of a fight makes you a sitting duck, regardless of how hard you've turtled.

MPING

ether it's a classic Cozy Campfire, or
pter 3's new Tent, camping is always a
t way to set up base, heal and recalibrate
en you've got a bit of downtime. Camping
a heal per second mechanic, and can be
red among your squadmates.

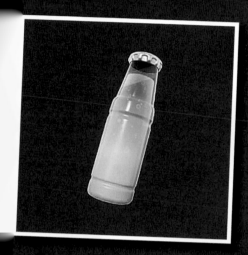

TIP!

Get Juiced! There's been an array
healing juices that pop up every n
and then, depending on the seaso
Guzzle Juice, Slurp Juice... be sure
check out what healing items are
play before you jump into a match

RESTORING SHIELDS

ee that little blue bar? That's your Shield
a bank of points that protect your HP by
bsorbing damage until it's depleted. Getting
Shield should be one of your top priorities
when you land on the island, and maintaining
t should be a constant goal throughout the
match. Seriously, Shields come in clutch when
you least expect them; you're always better
with than without.

SMALL SHIELD POTION

Also known as Minis, these grant 25 Shield
Points, with a cap of 50. They can't fully
generate a Shield but they can be used super
quickly (they only have a two second usage
time) so they're perfect for mid-battle usage
to recover damage taken.

SHIELD POTION

Also known as Big Pots, these grant 50 Shield
Points, all the way up to the Shield Points
max 100. Because they take five seconds
to use, they're best suited to non-combat
consumption, or if you have really strong
cover during a battle.

FOOD

You can also look to the island itself to provide some sustenance on your travels. Foraging for food is a great way to get a quick pick-up for your Health and Shields. Their effects are immediate, they have a super quick usage rate (usually one second): pick 'em up, chow 'em down, and get going.

APPLES

Apples heal 5 HP and can be found in orchards, or any area with trees.

BANANAS

Bananas also heal 5 HP, but they can be found in warmer climates, near palm trees.

CABBAGES

Cabbages are a little mightier as they heal 10 HP, and can be found in farmland.

COCONUTS

Coconuts heal 5 HP/Shield, and can be found in more tropical areas, near palm trees.

CORN

Like cabbages, corn heals 10 HP and can also be found in farmland. Destroy some crops to find some.

MEAT

Meat is a little different in that it isn't foraged so much as hunted - strike down any of the island's wildlife to get some (check out the Wildlife chapter on p. 22-23 for more details). It heals 15 HP when consumed.

MUSHROOMS

Mushrooms are a valuable foraging find because they grant 5 Shield upon eating. The best part? Unlike potions, they don't have a cap - you can guzzle them all the way to a full shield. You can find them growing in shady areas of swamps and forests.

PEPPERS

Perhaps the most useful of the foods, peppers heal 5 HP and also grant a 20% movement speed boost for 60 seconds.

SLURPSHROOMS

Slurpshrooms are basically mushrooms+, granting 10 HP/Shields. You can find them in swampy areas of the island.

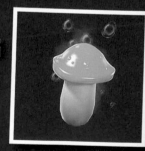

TIP!

Keep an eye out for Produce Boxes scattered across the map - these are filled with fruits and veg for you to munch down on without having to forage.

FISHING

Since fishing was introduced in Chapter 2, it's brought a whole new side to the Battle Royale match. But it's not just about kicking back and filling out your Collection Book; fishing actually is a super useful mechanic when it comes to Health. How? It's all about the fish.

Fish are some of the most efficient healing items in game, particularly in a pinch. Like most foraged foods, they only take one second to consume, but fish have way more gain than the comparably measly offerings from fruit and veg. Check out The 3 Basics: Surviving - Fishing on p. 24-25 for a deeper dive into fish and their healing properties.

SHARING IS CARING

If you're playing with a squad, you're going to want to keep an eye out for everyone's Health - not just yours. Chapter 3 has put more of a focus on teamwork, with more gameplay elements for more than one player (such as revival being quicker in a team, or doors that require more than one player to open), and that came with more multi-target healing options.

Campfires, Tents, Bandage Bazookas, Med Mist, Shield Kegs, Chug Splash... even Pizza Parties - there are always ways to take care of both yourself and your friends when playing Fortnite.

THE 3 BASICS:
SURVIVING - WILDLIFE

Back in Chapter 1, it was just you and the other 99 players trying to hunt you down roaming loose on the island. But since Chapter 2, the island's population began to grow, and now in Chapter 3, it is well and truly teeming with life - the wild kind.

Wildlife is an AI that roams around the island. Some are harmless and are there for you to brutally slaughter, and others are harmful and there to brutally slaughter you. When it comes to the wild, you can either:

- **Hunt Them:** Slain wildlife will drop meat, which can be consumed for 15 HP.

- **Tame Them:** Meat can also be used to tame other animals. Tamed animals will fight alongside the player in battles.

- **Ride Them:** Sometimes a regular vehicle just won't do the trick. Introduced in Chapter 3, Season 3, players can ride certain tamed animals across the island.

THE WILD AND WONDERFUL

Just like everything else on the island, the wildlife chops and changes season by season. Sometimes a species is in, another time it's out.

This is Fortnite, of course, so a weird and wonderful array of wildlife have made appearances (like raptors, alien parasites and klombos), but here are the, uh... more mainstream of the recurring cast of critters.

CHICKENS

Chickens usually flee from the player, but they drop meat if you manage to catch one. If you grab one and hold it above your head when jumping, it provides a kind of float effect and slows your fall.

BOARS

Boars will attack a player, or flee if they're attacked first. They drop both meat and mushrooms if they're hunted. The player can tame them as allies in combat, or to ride them across the map.

Type	Location
Hostile	Woodlands and farmlands

Type	Location
Passive	Near farms, corn fields

FROGS

These passive water-dwellers will flee the player, and it's a tough task to try to catch them once they get bouncing. However, if you do catch one, it'll drop meat.

WOLVES

Wolves will attack on sight and usually spawn in packs of three or more. They can be hunted for meat, but they can also be tamed. They will fight alongside the player, or can be ridden as a vehicle.

Type	Location
Passive	Riverside and near water

Type	Location
Hostile	Riverside and near water

THE 3 BASICS:
SURVIVING - FISHING

Mechanics have come and gone, but ever since its introduction at the start of Chapter 2, fishing has proven that it isn't a fad. So, if you want to survive out there on the island, you're going to have to know your way around a fishing rod for sure.

When fishing was first introduced, there were only three types of fish to catch. Ah, simpler times. Now, it's a whole, thriving ecosystem, teeming with different ways for you to boost your health, gain thermal vision and complete another entry in your Collection Book.

FISHING GEAR

The first thing you need to do in order to fish is find a spot. You can fish in any calm waters, but the best places are active Fishing Spots (look out for the bubbling white circle on the water surface). Fishing Spots are all around better: better fish, better loot, better odds. With your spot fixed, you'll need your tools:

- **Fishing Rod (Common):** Fishing rods spawn in barrels and on the ground, nearby fishing spots.

- **Pro Fishing Rod (Rare):** Pro Fishing Rods have a better chance to find rarer fish and loot. They spawn in the same places as regular rods, and you can also get one through by upgrading.

- **Harpoon Gun (Rare):** The Harpoon Gun is a short-range weapon, but can only be used in active Fishing Spots.

- **Explosives:** Want to make your fishing a little more extreme? Shoot a Fishing Spot with a rocket to get a quick (and extreme) payout.

CATCH OF THE DAY

Fish are not immune to the whims of the devs' Vaulting. The deepsea denizens that swim beneath the island's waters often change depending on the season, but the usual suspects are as follows:

Floppers are Uncommon and can be found almost everywhere across the island. You can carry up to 4, and they heal 40 HP (up to 100 HP). They have a size range of 30-60 cm.

Jellyfish are Rare catches. You can carry up to 3. They heal 20 HP/Shield to the player that consumes it and surrounding players.

Spicy Fish are Rare fish. You can carry up to 3, and they can heal 15 HP and bestow a one minute speed boost. They have a size range of 30-60 cm.

Hop Floppers are Epic fish. You can carry up to 3, and they heal 25 HP (up to 75 HP). They have a whopping size range of 5-100 cm.

Cuddle Fish are Rare fish that deal 35 HP worth of damage to any enemy they can cuddle. You can carry up to 6, and they have a size range of 35-70cm.

Slurpfish are Epic fish that are more commonly found in Fishing Spots than calm waters. You can carry up to 3, and they heal 40 HP/Shield. They have a size range of 30-60 cm.

Shield Fish are Rare. You can carry up to 3, and they heal 50 Shield. They have a size range of 35-65 cm.

Small Fry are Common catches. You can carry up to 6, and they heal 25 HP (up to 75 HP). They have a size range of 15-25 cm.

Stink Floppers are Uncommon catches that can be used as projectile weapons. They create a cloud of toxic gas that deals 5 damage per tick. You can carry up to 3, and they have a size range of 35-70cm.

CATCH 'EM ALL

There's a lot more than just fish deep down in those pools of blue, you know. Cast your fishing rod and see if you can pull up a weapon or two, some ammo... or another Rusty Can.

TIP!
Love fish but hate fishing? Be sure to raid cooler boxes and ice machines, you may find a flopper.

QUITE THE COLLECTOR

Use your Collection Book to keep an eye on all of your fishing feats! This book shows all the fish you collect through the current season, with stats on the amount you've caught, your personal best size catch, and a comparison to your friends'.

THE 3 BASICS:
SURVIVING - CHARACTERS

You've never been alone on the Battle Royale island thanks to the 99 other players out there gunning for your head, but over the years, Epic has been populating the island with more and more AI characters than ever. Some are there to help, some are there to, well, also gun for your head. But hey, you'll never know unless you take the time to chat.

With Chapter 3, Characters are no longer involved in distributing Quests (see more about those on p. 38-39), but they've still got their fair share of business to be going about in the middle of a death match. Let's get to know the island dwellers a little bit better.

TIP!
Did you know that Characters weren't always hanging around? They were first introduced back in Chapter 2, Season 5. The very first Character was Bandolette, the jungle predator.

TIP!
You'll know you're close to a Character when a speech bubble icon appears on your map.

FINDING FRIENDS AND FOES

Characters can be found all across the map, and their location usually changes season by season. It's always a good idea to check online for the latest location updates for existing NPCs, as well as learning about the new faces that have touched down on the island.

While no Characters stack up on each other's spawn points, there are a few that tend to spawn around the same area as each other. In this case, usually only one of them will spawn per match. Oh, and don't forget - NPCs spawn once per match, so if another player has hired or taken them out first, then they're gone for that whole round.

If you're lucky enough to reach an NPC first, then you'll be able to interact with them. Each character has their own possible interactions, and while the developers are known to mix things up each season, the usual options are as follows:

- **Duel:** Challenge the Character to a fight, and win their weapon (and Gold) in reward.

- **Hire:** Recruit them to fight by your side.

- **Prop Disguise:** They'll turn you into a prop, but the cover will break when you take damage or use an item.

- **Rift:** Have a Character open up a rift to teleport you into the sky, ready to deploy your glider. This is a great way to quickly cover ground in a pinch.

- **Storm Forecast:** Get a heads up on where the next Storm phase will form.

- **Tip Bus Driver:** Exactly what it says on the tin, sweetie.

- **Weapon:** Buy a weapon from the Character.

TIP!
For more information on duelling NPCs, be sure to check out Winning the 1v1: PvE on p. 35!

TIP!
Just as the line-up changes every season, it always varies in size. Some seasons have added a ton of new NPCs to the island, while others have scaled the roster down in favour of other seasonal gameplay mechanics.

GOLD TALKS

You can't always expect everyone to open up for free; some NPCs may be there to help, but they've got to make a living too. Characters accept payment in the form of Gold Bars, a special type of in-match currency that you can use to purchase items, services or intel. You can find Bars all across the island, like opening safes, destroying items such as cash registers and beds, completing bounties, and our tried and trusted favourite: looting the corpse of the player you so graciously just ended.

CHARACTER COLLECTION BOOK

You can visit the Character Collection Book in the lobby to see which Characters you've stumbled across so far, or who you should be seeking out if you're trying to get a full set.

THE 3 BASICS:
SURVIVING - WEAPONS

Never has 'last but certainly not least' been more fitting than introducing the last branch of survival mastery: weapons. Yes, you can make it to the Storm's final phase with some pacifist decision making and impressive mobility, but you're going to need to understand weapons in order to take down the remaining few players and snatch the crown for last man standing.

Fortnite's arsenal of weaponry is diverse, to say the least, and it's unlikely that anyone will know the entire roster season by season, stat by stat. But there's a bigger picture when it comes to weapons that makes it easy to categorise all the new arrivals, unvaulted classics and arsenal mainstays: ammo, rarity, upgrades, and of course (the big one) weapon types.

WEAPON AMMO

If it's not a melee weapon, it's going to need some ammo to actually deal any damage. Each weapon type in Fortnite has different ammo requirements.

It's pretty easy to get your hands on ammo: you can find it in chests, ammo boxes, supply drops, and sometimes even just out in the open for anyone to walk right through and pick up. Your max ammo capacity is all the way up at 999, so if you see some, grab some. When it comes to ammo, it's always better to finish with more than you needed than to die without.

	Ammo Type	Weapon Type	Damage Per Shot	Effective Range
	Light Ammo	Pistols, SMGs	Low	Close
	Medium Ammo	Pistols, Assault Rifles	Medium	Mid
	Heavy Ammo	Sniper Rifles	High	Long
	Shells	Shotguns	High	Close
	Rockets	Explosives	Very High	Mid/Long

*There are other ammo types, like Arrows and Energy, but the corresponding weapons are often season-specific or vaulted.

WEAPON RARITY

Weapons have the same six-tiered rarity hierarchy that all other cosmetics and items in Fortnite fall under. A weapon's rarity indicates both its power and your chances of finding it in a match. Generally, the rarer the weapon, the stronger. For example, a Common Assault Rifle will deal 30 damage per shot, but a Legendary Assault Rifle deals 36. Rarer weapons also have shorter reload times.

TIP!

You won't be able to find Mythic or Exotic weapons on the map. Mythic weapons are wielded by enemy NPCs (see Winning the 1v1: PvE on p. 35 for more info), and you'll need to cough up some Gold Bars to friendly NPCs (check out Surviving - Characters on p. 25-27) to get your hands on Exotic weapons.

Common	Uncommon	Rare	Epic	Legendary	Mythic	Exotic

While it's natural to assume that rarer weapons are better, it's important not to get too caught up in the tier system when making your loadout judgments. Certain weapons are better to have than others, regardless of their rarity, due to their versatility in combat. You'll want to keep a balanced weapon selection for as long as you can. You don't want to be out there tossing a Common Sniper Rifle to the trash in order to fit another Legendary Pistol in your loadout - that Pistol isn't going to have your back when a player starts sniping you from across the field, Legendary or not. Weapon type and weapon range should always be considered before weapon rarity - just remember: balance!

WEAPON UPGRADES

Thanks to Chapter 2, weapon rarity is no longer fixed and can be increased, provided you have the Gold Bars necessary to amp up your arsenal's firepower. There are two methods of upgrading a weapon, and usually they are mutually exclusive; the Epic devs like to switch between methods during seasons, so be sure to check online to see which is the current way for you:

Don't worry, this town's plenty big for the two of us. Llamas love sharin'!

REVOLVER
(UNCOMMON)
STOCK: 4
BUY   0 / 25

UPGRADE BENCHES

These can be found all across the island (more prevalently in POIs and key landmarks). They allow players to upgrade weapons in exchange for Gold Bars. The higher the rarity, the higher the cost.

NPC SERVICES

Depending on your season, certain Characters can upgrade your weapons for a certain Gold Bar fee, too.

TIP!

Thrifty Tip! While it's not technically 'upgrading', you can also get your hands on some high rarity weapons using Vending Machines, if you manage to find one. Their 50 Gold Bar cost is way lower than the 200+ that's required with Upgrade Benches or NPCs.

Rarity Upgrade	Cost (Gold Bars)
Common → Uncommon	200
Uncommon → Rare	300
Rare → Epic	400
Epic → Legendary	500

WEAPON TYPES

The Epic devs certainly haven't been shy to introduce a plethora of new weapons to the battle arena, even giving appearances to some of the most iconic weapons in pop culture (like the Star Wars lightsaber). But no matter how plentiful (or outlandish) the weapons may be, they can usually be sorted into one of the eight categories that have been around since Day 1.

ASSAULT RIFLES

Assault Rifles are meant for medium to long range combat. With a high damage output, they're one of the best balanced weapons the game has to offer. These are hitscan weapons, which means there's no travel time to consider; any shot taken will immediately connect with its target, provided the aim was on point.

TIPS!

- Assault Rifles often have first shot accuracy, which means its first fired shot doesn't have any bloom. Use this opportunity to take a headshot, then switch to body to accommodate for the bloom.

- Don't try to use these at close range - they have a low hipfire accuracy and don't always have the fastest fire rate.

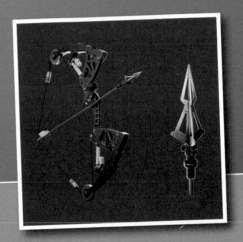

CROSSBOWS/BOWS

Crossbows and Bows are a rarer sight as they often spend more of their time in the Vault than on the island, but hey, who knows what a cheeky developer feels like sneaking back in? As projectile weapons, they require predictive tracking when aiming.

TIPS!

- Crossbows are unique in the Fortnite arsenal because they don't require ammo pickups to reload.

- Bows do not have fall-off damage, so a shot will deal the same damage at any distance.

EXPLOSIVES

Similar to Crossbows/Bows, Explosives are projectiles, and require tracking. All Explosives deal splash damage, which means it will also deal damage to a small radius around the projectile's landing spot. While they have a range of effect, they're best utilised at long distance.

TIPS!

- There's no better weapon type to disrupt builds or structures than with Explosives.

- Don't go playing with an Explosive too close range - they have friendly fire, which means you can be damaged by its blast, too.

PISTOLS

Pistols are a great pick-up - they'll get the job done, but you'll want to find something more specialised ASAP. Each weapon in this category vary quite widely in their use: some are specifically for close range (with good hipfire and a high fire rate) and others are better for closing distance (with slow fire rate and low damage drop off).

TIPS!

- Be sure to check out what Pistol you have before you equip it due to the weapon's wide range variety.

- Pistols that use Light Ammo have great hipfire accuracy.

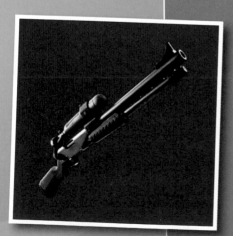

SHOTGUNS

Shotguns are devastating at close range, with a high DPS (damage per second) and forgiving area of effect. While they reign supreme up close, they pay for it with damage drop off - it can be hard to make use of one even just at mid range.

TIPS!

- Duellers swear by their Shotguns, so you'll need one if you're taking on any 1v1.

- Need to keep shooting? Keep your ammo topped up regularly, because partial reloads are faster than full reloads.

SNIPER RIFLES

No loadout is complete without a Sniper Rifle. These guns dominate the long-range field, dealing a deadly amount of damage. The trade-off? They can be difficult to wield, as their efficiency relies purely on a player's tracking ability and aim.

TIPS!

- You need to consider bullet speed and drop with Sniper Rifles, so if you're aiming at a moving target, aim slightly ahead of them.

- Sniper Rifles don't have any fall-off damage, so they deal the same damage at any distance. Essentially, you can down a player with two shots at any range, if you aim right.

SUBMACHINE GUNS (SMGS)

SMGs were built for short to medium range combat; the closer, the better. They have a great DPS and excellent hipfire accuracy, which makes them monsters up close. Unfortunately, they compensate with a high damage drop off and bullet spray, so they're pretty useless from further than mid-range.

TIPS!

- Try to shoot in controlled bursts in order to keep on top of the amount of ammo you're using.

- SMGs are great to combo with other weapons in duels. Use another weapon to close the distance and an SMG up close to finish them off.

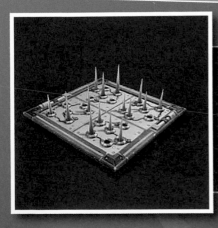

TRAPS

Traps are unique in that they are intended for build combat and defence. Players can lay them down to protect a stronghold, or try to trip up a pursuer in a build battle. Traps can be placed in any direction or orientation upon a structure.

TIP!

Iconic weapons from pop culture are categorised as Collaboration Weapons. These are usually super powerful, but thankfully very rare and very often Vaulted for their own good (may we be free of the Infinity Gauntlet's reign of tyranny and terror for good, amen).

WINNING THE 1V1: PVP

There's nothing quite like the frantic, pure, chaotic energy of a 1v1 duel. This is a core mechanic of Fortnite's gameplay loop - unless you get super lucky and let other players and the Storm take out all of your opponents, you're going to need to stare down at least one enemy and fight for the win.

OPTIMISE YOUR LOADOUT

When you're locked in a 1v1, you're not going to have time to readjust your loadout or make any major changes. You'll want to keep on top of it throughout the match in order to be well-prepared for any sudden gunfire. The optimal set-up is 2 Weapons - 2 Heals - 1 Dealer's Choice. Prioritise getting your hands on an Assault Rifle and smaller healing items (like Small Shield Potions and Bandages) so you can heal quickly if you take damage mid-fight.

KEEP MOVING

Don't let yourself be a sitting target. Keep your APM high and throw off their tracking by keeping your movement unpredictable.

ALTITUDE OVER ALL

Star Wars got it right all those years ago: the high ground advantage can't be beat. It's way easier to aim and shoot downwards than it is to shoot up, especially when we're talking landing headshots. Don't hesitate to build yourself up to more advantageous grounds during battles.

SHOOT, BUILD, REPOSITION, REPEAT

Learn this mantra; live by this mantra. Breathe this mantra. Take your shot, build a wall to shield and then reposition yourself before doing the whole thing again. You might need to adapt things depending on the fight scenario (don't bother building for a long-distance snipe; it'll only alert layers to your location), but it's key to know for most 1v1s.

WINNING THE 1V1: PVE

There's more to worry about than other players now. Chapter 2 introduced AI to the island and it has stayed just as hostile ever since.

HENCHMEN

There's usually some form of evil entity trying to take over the island - from GHOST and SHADOW to the Imagined Order, there's always something threatening in the background while you're busy dealing with all the other Battle Royale curveballs. Every evil organisation has its underlings ready to do its bidding: enter the henchmen (or forces. You know - evil organisation's pick).

TIP!

Random movement works particularly well on AI enemies because their tracking usually isn't great at predicting movement.

You can usually find them patrolling certain POIs. If a henchman spots you, a question mark will pop up over their heads, and if they're ready to fight, it'll change to an exclamation. Their AI isn't all that, so treat an encounter with them in the same way you would a relatively non-threatening PvP duel.

BOSSES

Bosses are considerably tougher than henchmen in that they have more HP, more Shields, and more reward if you manage to take them down.

- Try to start the battle from a distance if you can. Most bosses have 400 Shield and 100 HP, so kicking things off with a few headshots is always a good opener.

- Clear out the henchmen first. You don't want them interfering and outnumbering you.

- Really skilled players use the Storm as their own weapon. Get the timing right and you can use the Storm to drain a boss' Health and hasten their downfall.

- Keep alert! Bosses only spawn once per match, and you won't be the only one looking for them. Other players might try to sneak in and snipe out both you and the boss.

PICK YOUR PLAYSTYLE

Battle Royale is ultimately a game of chance - whether your landing spot happens to be the first on the Storm's hit list, or the only other players left finish each other off and leave you with the crown. You can prepare, but there's very little in your control once the match starts. There is one thing you can control, however: your playstyle.

Fortnite is a versatile game that has proven since its debut in 2017 that there's no one way to win a Victory Royale. You can try going in there guns a blaze, you can try building right to the skybox while the battle blazes beneath you, or you can pay a Cat-man hybrid to turn you into a bush to avoid your enemies. It's time to pick your playstyle.

THE CLASSIC

A classic player is a Jack of All Trades who wants to try it all, a player that will use all of the game's offerings without hyper-focusing on any one in particular. This is the quintessential Fortnite experience: balancing a loadout, dabbling in some fishing, engaging in some gun fights and building when necessary.

This playstyle is the perfect pick for new players looking to find out what Fortnite's all about, and more seasoned players who enjoy a more casual playstyle.

THE ASSASSIN

Assassins drop onto the map, find a weapon and start taking names. They work with a weapon-heavy loadout, no-scope like it's no big deal and always have the high ground advantage. When it comes to play objectives, Assassins are all about that sweet elimination XP bonus (in which they are constantly swimming, of course) and Bounty system.

This playstyle is well suited for those with experience in FPS games, as it relies heavily on player mechanics. As such, it has a high skill ceiling that requires a lot of practice to execute with the ruthless efficiency the Assassin calls for.

THE ARCHITECT

You can't find building mechanics like Fortnite's in any other Battle Royale game, so it makes sense that some players focus their entire playstyle around this unique system. An Architect's true weapon is their blueprint and 2B: they take on duels with the ability to manipulate it to their whim with guns as a secondary option. They'll force the battle into the sky or build a bridge and get out of there in a flash.

Like the Assassin, the Architect playstyle has a very high skill ceiling. It requires just as much practice to become a building master, so get to honing your craft in Creative until it's muscle memory.

THE MEDIC

A Medic player is a playstyle that really only works in a squad. This role sees the player focus on support, working with a healing-heavy loadout with plenty of multi-target healing items (or fish, if the Med Mist and whatnot are Vaulted), leaving all the heavy gun-toting to the rest of the team.

Chapter 3 really made this playstyle more viable, with certain supportive actions (like reviving Knocked players or starting a Reboot van) getting a boost with more players. The Medic is a good choice for those who want to play with friends but aren't a huge fan of duelling.

THE PACIFIST

Hey, sometimes players just want to outrun the Storm, dodge aggro NPCs and take in the sights of the island for as long as they can. Pacifists actively avoid duels, utilising survival and stealth skills. You'd be surprised how effective a Pacifist run can be, simply playing it safe to the top 10 and then taking out the final players within the last bubble.

This playstyle is best suited for players who really want to explore the island more and try their hand at all of the new features and mechanics that Fortnite introduces every season. It's also great for those more focused on non-Battle Royale objectives, like filling out Collection Books or completing Quests.

QUESTS

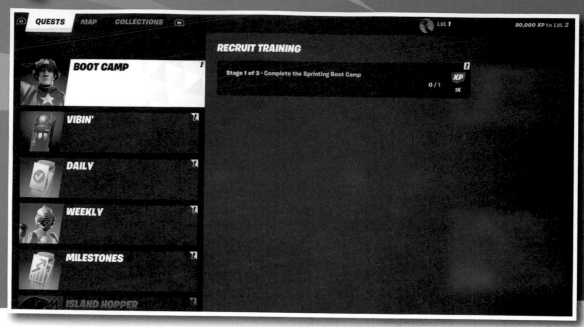

Since Chapter 3, quests have moved from being initiated on the island via NPCs to being found on a separate page from the Lobby.

They may have relocated, but they're just as important as ever. Quests are the fastest way to rack up XP to funnel into your Battle Pass.

DAILY QUESTS

Daily Quests are usually quick little tasks that are easy enough to do multiple of to make decent XP gains. They'll range from trivial things like eating apples and bananas to dealing damage with a Motorboat. Players are assigned three at once, with new quests replacing completed ones. Even though they don't give a lot of XP, completing enough will earn you a Daily Bonus Goal which deals out a lot more.

TIP!

Did you know? Quests originally had a rarity hierarchy (like everything else in Fortnite), but they were dropped when Chapter 3 debuted.

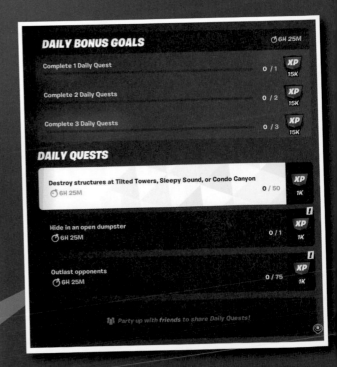

WEEKLY QUESTS

Weekly Quests (also known as Season Quests) are delivered weekly (duh), and are usually a little more of an ask than the Dailies - usually a little more risky. Sometimes you'll have to jump through flames in a vehicle, other times you'll need to visit certain spots or get eliminations with a certain weapon.

TIP!

Get by with little help from your friends! Squadding up with another player allows you to both receive XP for the completed quests.

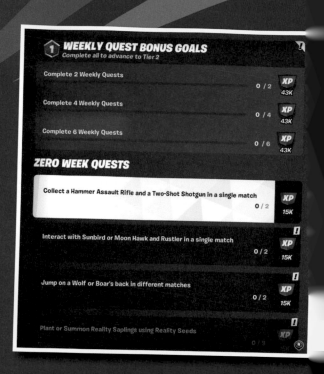

MILESTONES

Milestones are quests that reward players for doing basic gameplay 'milestones' within matches. Essentially, they're rewards for players exploring the island and expanding their game knowledge. A lot of these 'tasks' (and that's a loose use of the word 'task') are things you'd do naturally, like searching Chests or thanking the bus driver (hey, manners pay). Players are also given a stage clearance bonus each time they complete a set.

TIP!

Psst! They might not seem super significant, but you can earn over 3,000,000 XP from completing all the Milestone Quests!

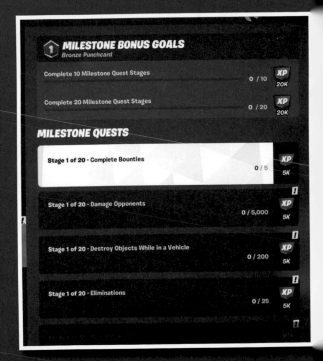

OTHER QUESTS

A lot of other quests will pop up, like Character quests, or storyline quests specific to the season (usually whichever evil faction is trying to run the island - you know, every evil regime has its to-do list). These can be for XP, but also for alternate Character skins and other goodies.

PRO SURVIVAL TIPS

So you've diligently poured over the last 40 pages or so, taking in all of the invaluable Fortnite knowledge and wisdom we have bestowed upon you. Here are some last minute tips to ensure you survive, thrive and arise as the last man standing.

PLAY AROUND THE STORM

- The Storm is more of a threat than ever due to the introduction of Storm Sickness in Chapter 3. It's no longer no big deal if you hang back for whatever reason and find yourself within the Storm. Storm Sickness means you'll take increased damage, so previous play tactics involving Storm play factoring into duels are no longer effective.

- When the Storm shrinks, don't be afraid to stay around its edges. Players tend to move as far into the middle of the Eye as they can; the fringes are always less populated. If you get in the clear early enough, you can also take cover and snipe out any approaching players running to safety.

COVER YOUR TRACKS

- Don't fully take a tree when harvesting - the disappearance animation can alert an enemy's attention, even from a distance.

- Close doors behind you. You weren't raised in a barn, right? An open door is a surefire sign that a player has been through, so cover your tracks.

STAY CAUTIOUS

- Be wary if you find signs of another player on your path. Open doors, open Chests, builds and broken walls are all signs that someone else has been (or still is) around. It's better to be safe than sorry.

- Stay in cover. Try not to run across an open area unless you have no other choice - you just don't know who has what vantage point and who can see you. It's way easier to strategise and play from cover, giving you the automatic upper hand.

- If you come across a big pile of kill-drop loot just left out on the ground, take a real quick pause. Someone clearly just died here, so check that the perpetrator isn't still lurking, hoping to lure you out with loot bait...

- ...And if you were the perpetrator, keep your guard up. There's a chance your little scuffle might have alerted nearby players to your location, so do a quick location scout before you start sifting through your spoils. If you're late game, you might even want to build around you while looting.

LISTEN UP

- Try to play with headphones instead of speakers. Headphones allow you to hear really subtle sounds like footsteps and other audio details.

- Be cautious of your own noise output - try to make as little noise as possible by walking or crouching when you've got company to get the jump on them.

- Switching and reloading weapons have specific audio cues for each weapon type. Once you've got enough gameplay experience under your belt, you may be able to recognise them and identify what your opponent is switching to.

SETTINGS FOR SUCCESS

- Give yourself the best chance of survival by ensuring your Settings are helping you, not hindering. Start by ensuring that Turbo Build/Builder Pro is enabled.

- Consider toggling Autorun depending on the situation. While you want to make as little noise as possible in close quarters, you may need to sprint across a long distance, and Autorun allows you to use the rest of your fingers free to check the map.

FORTNITE MAZE

Help Jonesy make his way through the island and avoid the perils to get that sweet Victory Crown! See answers on p. 62-63.

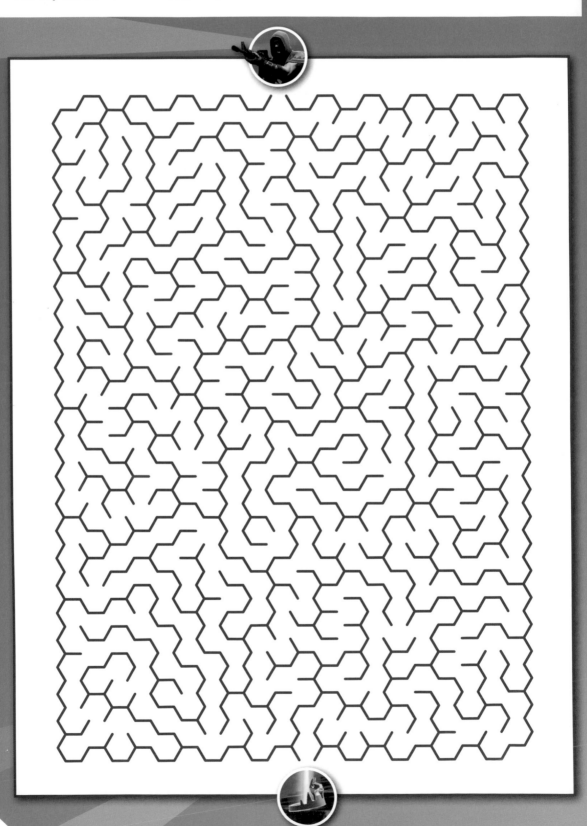

WORDSEARCH

Can you find the Fortnite Characters in the wordsearch below? See p. 62-63 for answers.

```
L O O P E L D D U C N D R A
T O M A T O H E A D S C C L
J R O N I N L I L W H I P C
E K G I N M C R Y P T I C G
L A G A H B E D G S S R N A
Y I T E L L R L H O K I K N
K I C J T A N A R A L Y I L
W I E S O E C B I K V K T L
A S U H C N O T C N T E U Y
H R I A E A E A I I I D N L
N Y L N B R U S L C W A B N
O H O T N Q H L Y I O A C I
O L C A A A B C G G U A C O
M A H T A E K A C N A M G H
```

Character Bank:

1. Jonesy
2. Ludwig
3. Brainiac
4. Cuddlepool
5. Guaco
6. Lil Whip
7. Mancake
8. Shanta
9. Haven
10. Galactico
11. Ronin
12. Rustler
13. Moon Hawk
14. Kyle
15. Bao Bros
16. Quackling
17. Cryptic
18. Tomato Head

THE ISLAND:
WELCOME TO ARTEMIS

Welcome to the arena! You'll get real familiar with this island real quick, as all of your Battle Royale matches will take place upon its varied and wonderful environments. Every great victor knows the lay of the land, particularly the land they plan to slay 99 other players on.

As Fortnite has now established, with a new chapter comes a new island. After Athena and Apollo, Chapter 3 brought us Artemis: initially an iced out scape, that has now thawed to reveal new features, new biomes, and new and familiar POIs.

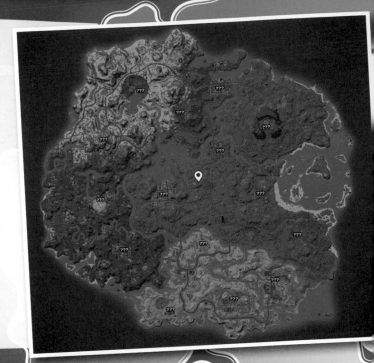

KEEP THINGS IN THE FAMILY

Did you know that Artemis is the Greek goddess of the hunt, the wild and the moon? She's also the twin sister of Apollo, the Chapter 2 island's namesake.

JUST RENTING

Artemis is just as ever-changing as its predecessors, with locations popping in and out (or getting completely reskinned) all across the island with different updates. You can also visit collaboration locations, like Marvel's the Daily Bugle.

HAVE WE MET BEFORE?

We may be on our third island, but certain POIs are just too iconic to let go of. Keep an eye out for old favourites like Tilted Towers, Shifty Shafts, Greasy Grove and Loot Lake across Artemis. They're not exact carbon copies, but the root is still there. Even the Daily Bugle is inside the classic Volcano.

WAS THAT ALWAYS THERE?

Be sure to keep an eye out when traversing the map, because the developers really like to hide little easter eggs throughout the island hinting at the next big update.

ISLAND DWELLERS

Remember, it's not just the other players you have to look out for on the island. Artemis is filled with different forms of life, with differing opinions on whether to let you keep yours. For more details, check out the Characters chapter on p. 26-27 and the Wildlife chapter on p. 22-23.

LANDING WITH STYLE

You know, there's a lot of truth in the whole "start as you mean to go on" thing. Your landing spot may seem like a throwaway decision, but it's surprisingly key to your potential eventual win in that match. Without the right consideration, you might be trashing that Victory Royale as soon as you leap from the Battle Bus.

Fortnite is a game that lets you experiment with a lot of the gameplay to let you find whatever style suits you best, but there's pretty much only one, inarguably best way to touch down onto the island, regardless of personal preference:

1. **Aim low:** Every descent from the Battle Bus consists of a skydive and a glide. Skydiving is a lot faster than gliding, so is preferable for speedy touch downs. For a fast descent, you want to delay your glider's deployment for as long as possible by aiming for lower ground to maximise your dive time. But then...

2. **Aim high:** Switch it up when your glider inevitably deploys, because you don't want to be a floating duck taking its time to hit the ground when you could steer it towards higher ground, touch down faster and get to finding your weapon ASAP. Not only does this give you a good lay of the land to see what you're dealing with, it also gives you automatic high ground advantage to deal with any players that landed in the same spot. Even if your landing spot doesn't have any huge vertical discrepancies, remember that a rooftop is always infinitely better than the middle of the street.

TIP!

It's not much, but you can speed up your glider's descent a little bit by strafing left to right, or aiming your camera at the ground and pressing forward.

PICK YOUR LANDING SPOT

While there may be one indisputably best way to land, there's not one indisputably best location. It's ultimately up to you (or your Quest requirements) as to where you want to start your island traversal, but here are some tips to keep in mind when it comes to the decision making:

- **Some Like it Hot:** Hot drops are popular spots for players to land, usually just whatever POI falls in line with the Battle Bus' drop-off route. They're popular for good reason, as they're usually pretty loot and resource heavy... but the trade-off is early skirmishes and battles are practically a given. Hot drops are great if you're looking to rack up a kill count quickly (just make sure you have an exit strategy ready if you can't get the upper hand), but if you want an easier landing, best avoid them.

- **Don't go too remote:** Be careful you don't veer too far in your avoidance, though. Landing in a random remote spot may be a safer option in terms of touch-down 1v1s, but you'll probably struggle to put together any decent loadout as good resources and loot tend not to plentifully spawn in the middle of nowhere. Sure, no enemies is great, but no resources? Not so great.

- **Balance:** Landing is a delicate balance between resources and safety. Hot drops are high risk, high reward; remote locations are low risk, low reward. If you're looking for something in the middle, try to get some distance from the Battle Bus route but still stick to landmarks, at least.

LAND, LOADOUT

Wherever you decide to land, your first priority should be attending to your loadout. Get out your pickaxe and start swinging to rack up mats, look out for potions and mushrooms to build up your Shield, and acquire your first weapons. If you've opted for a hot drop, you'll want something close-range like a Shotgun to deal with nearby players.
If you're somewhere more remote, you'll be wanting to secure yourself a mid/long range gun like a Rifle before you get moving.

MAP MOBILITY

You've leapt off the Battle Bus, nailed your landing, got a promising loadout and are ready to start exploring the island. There's a lot of ground to cover, a lot of enemies to avoid and a lot of Storm to outrun - luckily, you're not expected to do it all with your feeble little human legs.

There have always been a multitude of interesting and creative ways to make your way across the map (from killer mech suits and loot sharks to shopping carts and flying saucers), so let's dive into looking at all the ways to boost your mobility.

BY LAND

Cars have become a mobility mainstay since their introduction in Chapter 2, Season 3. Chapter 3 kept them around, but they're a little less hardy, as they take more damage from explosives than before. All cars spawn with 40-100 fuel.

TIP!

Of all of Fortnite's offerings, vehicles seem to zoom in and out of the Vault the most. Be sure to check the patch notes for your current season to see which vehicles have been introduced or survived last season's cull.

ISLANDER PREVALENT

- Seats: 4 • HP: 800

The Prevalent is the most commonly found across the island. It comes in three variations: the Prevalent, the Prevalent GG2020 and a taxi. It is best suited for on-road driving.

VICTORY MOTORS WHIPLASH

- Seats: 2 • HP: 800

The Whiplash is a sports car with a boost function to spend fuel for extra speed. Its Mark 51 variant has unlimited fuel.

OG BEAR

- Seats: 4 • HP: 1000

The OG Bear is a medium speed car with two seats in the front and two in the truck. It's best suited for off-road driving.

TITANO MUDFLAP

- Seats: 2 • HP: 1,200

The Mudflap (also known as a Semi or Big Rig) is a slow-speed vehicle that is best suited for on-road driving.

TIP!

Don't forget! You can repair cars by parking them near a lit Cozy Campfire, or by using a Repair Torch.

BY WATER

Much more of the current island is covered in the blue stuff than its very first iteration, but there aren't all that many ways to traverse across it. Sure, every now and then the developer's toss us a Loot Shark to ride or similar, but there's really only been one mainstay marine vehicle.

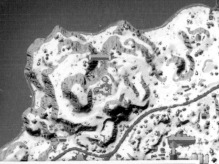

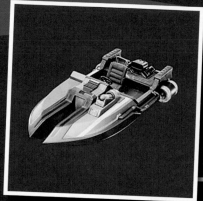

MOTORBOAT   • Seats: 4   • HP: 800

Motorboats are water vehicles armed with single-shot missiles. They can travel on water regardless of stream flow, and have a boost function that can gain them a lot of speed. If you really want, you can ride them on land, but they lose 1 HP per second (or 2 HP if you boost).

BY AIR

While the CHOPPA spends a lot of its time circling in and out of the Vault, there are way more efficient ways to travel through the island's airspace.

TIP!

Sometimes a regular vehicle just won't do the trick. Introduced in Chapter 3, Season 3, players can ride certain tamed animals across the island. Check out the Wildlife chapter on p. 22-23 for more details.

ZIPLINE

Ziplines have been a feature since Chapter 1, Season 7. They give players a quick mobility boost from Point A to Point B while still allowing access to weapons and items. Chapter 3, Season 3 also introduced a new form of vertical zipline called Ascenders.

While they're certainly useful for fast travel, they do make you somewhat of a sitting duck, so if an enemy spots you mid-zip, be ready to drop off at any point to disrupt your predicted trajectory and throw them off. Same if someone decides to hop on behind you and you find yourself with an unexpected plus one. Don't worry! There's no fall damage when dropping from ziplines, so don't be afraid to drop it like it's hot if necessary.

LAUNCH PAD

Launch Pads let you launch yourself into the sky, deploy your Glider and sail on out of there. It's a great way to gain some quick verticality in order to sail out of harm's way, be it another player or even the approaching Storm.

Launch Pads can be used by anyone on the map, so be sure that the opponent you were trying to escape from hasn't jumped and glided right on after you. Don't let your guard down until you're sure you're in the clear.

THE GOOD OLD DAYS

Fortnite has cycled its way through a ridiculous amount of vehicles (and yet no actual cycles, strangely enough) over the years. If you miss the mobility options from when you first started playing, or you want to try this fabled Quadcrasher that was before your time, then dig into the vehicular Vault in Creative mode to dust off some of the classics.

TIP!

Opt for a hitscan gun when ziplining - they're the easiest to use while moving.

CROSSWORD

See answers on p. 62-63.

ACROSS

4. You can only get this weapon type from enemy NPCs.

5. Fortnite's genetically modified vegetable.

7. The most effective range for light ammo and shells.

14. This weapon type deals splash damage.

16. Using ADS for a brief second before shooting.

17. This playstyle is best suited to those who like to build.

18. A cheaper method of upgrading weaponry.

19. The vertical zipline variant introduced in Chapter 3, Season 3.

21. You need this to tame an animal.

23. When you're down, but not out.

24. The owner of a house with a basketball court.

DOWN

1. Multi-target healing fish.

2. This weapon type doesn't have any fall off damage.

3. Your best bet when it comes to ascension.

6. Everyone's favourite cat-muscle man hybrid.

8. The name of the Chapter 3 island.

9. This consumable grants a speed boost.

10. The only flammable mat.

11. The worst type of catch.

12. The type of weapon to use on a zipline.

13. These fish are best used as projectiles.

14. You can only get this weapon type from friendly NPCs.

15. The character that ended Chapter 2, played by Dwayne "The Rock" Johnson.

20. The Marvel collab POI that ushered in Chapter 3.

22. Our first location in every match.

18

MAKING PROGRESS

There's more to Fortnite than just the Victory Crown. The real game goes way beyond just the match results; the bigger picture is all about the progress you make. There are different systems to keep track of all your progress in different aspects of the game.

THE BATTLE PASS

The Battle Pass is an in-game system that allows players to trade in XP in exchange for cosmetic rewards. It changes each season, offering new treats, like skins, emotes, gliders and even pickaxes. There are two versions of the Battle Pass: the full, paid version, and a free version that offers fewer rewards, but doesn't cost any V-Bucks to acquire.

1. **Linear Progress (XP):** This the most used method, probably because it's the most simple. Players earn XP by playing the game, and the XP is directly funneled into the Pass, earning rewards as you hit certain numbers.

TIP!

You don't need to crack open your virtual wallet to get the best cosmetics! You can make enough V-Bucks to purchase a full Battle Pass with the free challenges if you're prepared to grind. Maxing out the Battle Pass also yields enough V-Bucks to buy the next season's pass.

2. **Selective Progress (XP, Battle Stars):** If Epic's feeling a bit spicy, sometimes Battle Stars are used as the Battle Pass currency. Players earn Battle Stars from gameplay, and they can then claim a reward from the ones on offer. It allows the player more freedom of choice, but there are some restrictions, such as cosmetics needing pre-requisite conditions to unlock.

XP

XP is key to leveling up, and can be obtained by playing regular matches, or completing specific quests or challenges. Whether your current season is using the Linear or Selective system, you're still going to need XP. Looking to boost your XP? Here are some tips:

QUESTS, QUESTS, QUESTS

Be sure to check the Quest page before each match so you can be efficient about how you're spending your match time. Making your way through the Quests can yield a huge amount of XP. For more information on Quests, check out p. 38-39.

SHARING TRULY IS CARING

Squad up! Use the Party Assist function to share the Quest workload among your teammates. 15 headshots just went down to five when you're in a trio.

VICTORY ROYALE

There's more to a Victory Royale than just bragging rights. Playing throughout the match gives you XP for certain actions, and per elimination, but the biggest regular play payout is for the number one spot.

TIP!

Don't dismiss the dailies! Daily Quests may offer less XP, but they're usually easy and quick to complete, which makes them a simple and swift add-on when it comes to payout.

HOW LONG WILL YOU SURVIVE?

Take a deep sigh of relief: you've covered the whole Battle Royale journey from where to land to getting that Victory Crown. You know how to fill your Battle Pass, and how to cast your fishing line. You know how to balance your loadout and how to turn yourself into a prop in disguise. Right? You do know all of this, right?

Time to test whether you've been paying attention! Take this quiz and check your answers on p. 62-63 to see how long you'll survive down on the island...

1 What type of ammo is required for close range weaponry?

a. Light

b. Medium

c. Rockets

2 What's a balanced, classic loadout option?

a. 2 Weapons - 2 Heals - 1 Dealer's Choice

b. 2 Weapons - 2 Heals - 2 Dealer's Choice

c. 1 Weapon - 3 Heals - 1 Dealer's Choice

7 What's the best way to recover HP during a duel?
a. Cozy Campfire
b. Bandages
c. Medkit

8 What's the best way to track an enemy's movement when shooting?
a. Shoot where they are
b. Shoot behind them
c. Shoot ahead of them

3 What is the 1v1 duel mantra?
a. Shoot, Reposition, Build, Repeat
b. Shoot, Build, Reposition, Repeat
c. Build, Shoot, Reposition, Repeat

9 Which wild animals are you likely to find near water?
a. Wolves and Frogs
b. Wolves and Boars
c. Chickens and Boars

4 What's the best weapon type to close the distance?
a. SMG
b. Pistol
c. Assault Rifle

10 What's the best fish to help you outrun the Storm and into the Eye?
a. Flopper
b. Spicy Fish
c. Cuddle Fish

5 You're trapped in a duel you aren't prepared for! What build do you use to make your escape?
a. Turtle
b. Ramp Rush
c. 90s

6 You've spotted an enemy mid zipline. What weapon type do you pull out of your arsenal?
a. Hitscan
b. Projectile
c. Melee

SPOT THE DIFFERENCE

Challenge! Okay, let's see just how good your powers of observation are. Take your time and study both the pictures below and try to find the eight differences between them. Answers on p. 62-63.

EMOTE CODEBREAKER

Time to get down! Can you crack the code and identify these popular Fortnite emotes? Answers on p. 62-63.

KEY

1	2	3	4	5	6	7	8	9	10	11	12	13
A	B	C	D	E	F	G	H	I	J	K	L	M

14	15	16	17	18	19	20	21	22	23	24	25	26
N	O	P	Q	R	S	T	U	V	W	X	Y	Z

1

3	8	9	3	11	5	14

2

26	1	14	25

3

6	18	5	19	8

4

2	15	14	5	12	5	19	19

5

16	21	18	5

19	1	12	20

6

4	1	2

7

15	18	1	14	7	5

10	21	19	20	9	3	5

8

23	9	7	7	12	5

9

6	12	15	19	19

10

18	1	13	2	21	14	3	20	9	15	21	19

59

A FRIEND LIKE FORTNITE

As one of the biggest games of all time, it makes sense that a lot of people want to get in on the action. Fortnite has boasted some of the most impressive collaborations in the gaming industry since the iconic Marvel's Avengers: Infinity War collab back in Chapter 1, Season 4, and there's no sign that Epic plans to stop baffling us with new additions any time soon. We've had rappers, gaming icons, cinema stars, superheroes, fashion brands and even LeBron James himself (it's about time, considering how often players have spent time at his house). Did you catch any of these Chapter 3 collabs live?

SUPERHERO TAKEOVER

Superheroes have long settled into the Battle Royale island, and even more touched down to Artemis than before. In fact, Chapter 3 began with a Marvel collaboration straight out the gate, with Spiderman's the Daily Bugle taking a prime spot as one of the first POIs on the new map.

But Spiderman wasn't the only super-powered guest this Chapter, as Doctor Strange, Scarlet Witch and Hawkeye also made appearances. Outside of the Avengers, players also got to unlock Rogue and Gambit skins as part of the X-Men collaboration. Who's the next superhero to make their designated Fortnite appearance? Are there even any left at this point?

SPORTS STARS

Epic also featured some of reality's superheroes, if you will, with a bunch of sports star collaborations. Tennis sensation Naomi Osaka dropped into the island in the Icon Series with her own skins and bundle, as well as the Naomi Osaka Cup in Competitive. Chapter 3 also saw the arrival of half-pipe queen and snowboarding champ Chloe Kim.

PLAY THAT MUSIC!

Party Royale may not have played as prevalent of a role in Fortnite's offerings in Chapter 3, but that didn't mean musicians didn't make it into the game. R'n'B duo Silk Sonic (Bruno Mars and Anderson .Paak) were the first musicians to join the Icon Series in Chapter 3. Epic also collaborated with hip-hop legends Wu-Tang Clan, bringing a style revolution to the island with Wu Wear items available in the store.

ALL HAIL THE GAMING ICONS

As a titan of the industry, Epic Games have always used Fortnite to showcase some of the most iconic characters in gaming, even from competing studios. League of Legends champion Vi finally made her appearance in Chapter 3 after her sister, Jinx, debuted in Chapter 2, Season 8.

Players also had the chance to play as the iconic action hero Nathan Drake from Naughty Dog's Uncharted series, as well as the one and only Ezio Auditore from Ubisoft's Assassin's Creed. If that wasn't enough, Epic also hooked in fighting game fans by collaborating once again with Capcom's Street Fighter, bringing Blanka and Sakura to the island after Chun-Li and Ryu made their debut in Chapter 2.

QUIZ ANSWERS

P42-FORTNITE MAZE

P43-WORDSEARCH

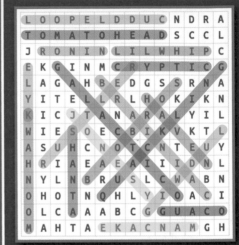

1. Jonesy	7. Mancake	13. Moon Hawk
2. Ludwig	8. Shanta	14. Kyle
3. Brainiac	9. Haven	15. Bao Bros
4. Cuddlepool	10. Galactico	16. Quackling
5. Guaco	11. Ronin	17. Cryptic
6. Lil Whip	12. Rustler	18. Tomato Head

P52/53-CROSSWORD